I0439323

Ignite Conversation!

By Julie Lucas

Copyright © 2014 **Authored By Name**
All rights reserved.

ISBN: 1497457122
ISBN 13:9781497457126
Library of Congress Control Number: **XXXXX (If applicable)**
LCCN Imprint Name: **City and State (If applicable)**

Acknowledgments

I want to thank those who have been the supportive people in my life.

My husband: Todrich Estelle.

My rock: Sabina Tomkins.

My light: Justin Tomkins.

Henry Feldman, Jennifer Dowd, Bernadette Foley, Ann Olson, Debra Nagel, Meg Moquete, and my parents, Luke and Donna Lucas.

I am a human being; I consider nothing that is
human alien to me.

Publius Terentius Afer
(195–159 BC)

Introduction

In 1992, I owned and managed The English School on University Way in Seattle, Washington. Students came from diverse places around the world such as China, Russia, Columbia, Spain, Ethiopia, Korea, Japan you name it. They had arrived in Seattle and needed to study English as their second language. Being a marketing guru, I was in touch with media agencies, such as the local radio and television stations, to promote my English school whenever possible.

When a truck full of explosives tore open the front of the Alfred P. Murrah building in downtown Oklahoma City and killed 168 people on April 20, 1995, my phone rang.

The media fabricated rumors linking Arabs and Muslims to the attack. The television stations wanted to know if I had any Arab students they could interview. I called my students from Yemen, Lebanon, and Libya, and asked if they would come to the school to be interviewed regarding the bombing in Oklahoma. I was told they needed to come as soon as possible, so their interviews could be aired in a timely fashion. My student from Yemen showed up right away. The camera technician and reporter showed up with their big bright lights.

The news anchors were reporting that the bombing was an Arab attack. I listened as they interviewed my student. The news anchors asked how my student felt living in a country where someone of Arab descent had attacked a state capitol. Would he return to his home country? I was appalled by the assumption that an Arab was at fault. I asked myself how the media shapes our ideas of who is guilty and who is innocent.

Eventually, Oklahoma congressman Dave McCurdy, who had propagated the rumor that there was a link between Oklahoma's Arab American population, Islamic groups, and the bombing, realized what he had started. The American public was all too eager to join in the inquisition. As it turned out, an American militia movement sympathizer and Gulf War veteran named Timothy McVeigh had detonated the explosive-filled Ryder rental truck parked in front of the building.

Many changes have occurred in the world since 1995. It is no longer valid to create a geographical separation between the East and the West. The Internet does not allow us to do that.

Taking a closer look at the history and the human suffering in other places in the world is important. Trying to understand another group of people in a historical context can bring us closer to positive relationships. Really listening to what people who live in other countries say about themselves is the beginning of a conversation hence the title of this book: *Ignite Conversation.*

Asking questions and expressing interest without judgment is moving toward acceptance; it's learning to accept one another for who we are. This is the direction the world needs to move in.

My first significant interaction with Saudi Arabia came through a Saudi student attending the University of Washington in Seattle. In the fall of 2010, I decided to rent out some rooms in my house in the Ravenna neighborhood of Seattle. Mr. Raed came to look at the room for rent. He spoke little English. He sat on my couch and asked many questions through a translator. He commented on the size of my house, saying it was too small. I thought I would never hear from him again. To my surprise, he moved into my house in October. I enjoyed his company, and we became friends.

During a rare snowstorm in Seattle, Raed wanted to walk to a friend's house, so I decided to accompany him. The wind was rough, blowing the fast falling snow around us wildly. We were struggling up a hill when he suddenly said I should be careful, because my uterus might fall out. He shocked and intrigued me with his ideas about women.

He, his friends, and his cousins were kind and respectful to me. I took on the role of the mother for him, but my daughter thought I was enabling his dependency on women. Whenever she got the chance, she challenged his ideas, and she refused to lift a finger for him when she knew he could do the task himself.

Simultaneously, an American man was also renting a room in the house. While Raed stayed up late to Skype with his family, the other renter stayed up equally late, enjoying the carefree and inebriated lifestyle of a young man who had recently turned twenty-one. Raed asked him and his friends why they wanted to drink so much; they asked him how he felt about not being able to.

Their relationship was amiable, but there was an undercurrent of confusion and chaos that would erupt from time to time with passionate protestations against the night-and-day cultural differences. Tobacco was the greatest glue.

Through Raed, I was introduced to a whole group of male Saudi students and discovered there are thousands of Saudis studying in the United States. There are so many of these students that they heavily influence Saudi culture. American culture has infiltrated Saudi Arabia. It is important to be aware of this fact. A report released by The International Educational Exchange explains that the number of Saudi exchange students have increased over the years. Statistics are provided on page 130.

As Americans our outlook is becoming increasingly global. We are connected to more and more countries through economic trade. Our international partnerships are more closely interrelated than ever before. This connection makes understanding one another more important than it was before; when we had the choice of remaining separate.

After many conversations with the Saudi young men who smoked their hookahs at my house, I decided to take a teaching job in Riyadh. At first, the idea seemed outrageous to those who knew me, because I am an independent woman. I love to ride my bike from place to place. I come and go as I please. I enjoy a glass or two of wine on occasion; I love movies, theatre, and concerts of all types. Why would I give this up?

The answer is economic freedom! What does that say about the American economy? What does it say about Saudi Arabia? Saudi Arabia provides an English-speaking woman with a bachelor's degree a free place to live, all expenses paid, and an interesting job. I am thankful for the opportunity.

As an avid reader and lover of literature, I had read *Women at Point Zero* by Nawal El Saadawi. When I heard the author of this book was teaching at the University of Washington (UW), not far from The English School on University Way, I dropped what I was doing and went to UW to find her. I waited for her in a small classroom, and when she arrived, I approached her and asked if I could sit in on her classes. She welcomed me with a warm, open smile and gave me permission to attend her classes. Sometimes I attended along with my two children.

El Saadawi spoke passionately of Arab women; she wanted her students to understand that Arab women are women like us mothers, daughters, wives, and professionals. She strongly believes that Arab women do not need to be "freed" by American women, and she expressed this in no uncertain terms.

One of El Saadawi's favorite analogies addresses the Arab woman's traditional head coverings. El Saadawi suggests that American women also cover their faces but in a different way than Muslims. Our mask of makeup hides our faces and is our cover up. The face we choose to show the world is not our own. A different cover the mask of makeup hides our faces.

I love this analogy, and I think she has a good point. We spend a lot of money on makeup. So many women I know won't leave their homes without "putting their faces on."

I admit that I have judged women of other cultures by my own American standards. I am now living in Riyadh, Saudi Arabia, and yes, wearing an *abaya* is new and sometimes difficult for me. It is also different. But strangely enough, though I oftentimes want to rip my *abaya* off, I also find it liberating in the sense of not having to think about what to wear.

The face covering known as the niqab, *the shoulder-to-toe black garment known as the* abaya, *and the* hejab, *the scarf that covers the hair and shoulders, that some Muslim women wear from head to toe.*

It is the religious law in Riyadh for women to cover from head to toe when going outside the home. Some Muslim women cover their hair with a *hejab*, some cover their whole face, but every woman must cover her body in black cloth.

It is my belief that what a woman wears should be her choice. Living in Riyadh has not changed that. What has changed is that I am more aware of the subtle ways that my fashion choices are not always choices. Both cultures objectify women in different ways.

As a woman in her late forties, I look back on the years of my twenties and thirties and think about how much time I wasted, seeking the approval of men and women regarding my appearance. I wish I had spent more time on developing other aspects of myself.

My parents and the society in which I lived encouraged me to focus on my looks. When I gained weight, I received instant negative feedback. Using my mind was not stressed as a positive goal to achieve.

I cannot judge a whole population of women by their clothing. It is their world, in which they live. I was not born into their culture; they can define who they are for themselves. As people from the Western world, we should listen to them. What are the women saying? I think if we listen, we will find that we are just a little bit closer to knowing the women behind the veils.

I have the privilege of knowing Arabs. The friendships I have formed consistently remind me that I must begin with looking at my own life before I judge others. I am a product of my environment, and this environment often asks me to view the world through an American national and cultural framework, which impacts how I view people from other places. Yet the amazing people I know in the Middle East are constant guides to the unknown; they kindly and gently show me other ways of viewing the world.

When I tell Americans that I live in Saudi Arabia, I am often asked why. This book stems from the desire to allow Americans to learn from Saudis as I have, and vice versa. Rather than a desire to simply explain my own experiences, I strive to open direct dialogue between women from the United States and those from Saudi Arabia. There is no substitute for conversation, nor for the lessons we can learn by temporarily suspending our own beliefs to see the world in a new way.

I am privileged to have such interactions every day, to learn from Arabs, and to share my own life story. I hope to give this experience to others through this book. I believe we can all benefit from knowing one another better.

In an attempt to open this dialogue, I have asked a variety of American and Saudi Arabian women to ask questions of each other. Some have chosen to give their names and information about themselves. Some have chosen to remain anonymous.

All of the Saudi women who have participated in this survey have chosen not to put their names to their opinions. Who are the Saudi women who have participated? How did I find them?

The women from Saudi Arabia who chose to ask and answer questions are women I have come in contact with while living in Riyadh, KSA. The American women are women I have known in my lifetime. They are professors, friends, colleagues, and family.

I am a blond, blue-eyed, American woman who does not cover her hair while living in the Kingdom of Saudi Arabia. I stand out as a Westerner. I live on a securely guarded compound in the city. The compound looks and feels like a ghost town, but is full of expats from all over the world who work at the National Guard Hospital.

Inside the compound we don't have to wear an abaya. There are two different worlds that exist for those who live on compounds. Most of my time off the compound is spent teaching at the College of Medicine at King Saud bin Abdulaziz University for Health and Sciences. Here, I have come to know my Saudi colleagues—professors, librarians, and administrators—some of who have voluntarily participated in this book's project. These are educated women with degrees from universities around the world.

The other groups of Saudi women involved are from my wide network of friends here in the Kingdom of Saudi Arabia—and their being acquainted with me tells you they are open to befriending an American. Also, the fact that the conversation is conducted in English tells you that the level of education of those who have participated is high. You will hear from a few students, but most are professional women working outside the home.

In the next section you will find the explanation of my quest. I sent this information and questionnaire to those whom I wanted to participate.

Arab Women: Voices to Be Heard

I am conducting this survey in order to dispel the myths that American women and Arab women both have about each other. I am an American woman who is open to knowing Arab women as human beings. Just because they live in such a different world than mine and that world does sometimes seem like another planet to me that does not mean we are so different. We have commonalities, and we are female. We are human we all have the capacity for emotional depth. I have been rewarded with warm, viable relationships with women just like me: mothers, daughters, and sisters. These relationships have had a profound effect on me. I have found joy in my relationships with the brilliant and kind women of Saudi Arabia, Yemen, Jordan, Syria, and Palestine.

We often project our values onto others we meet. I am asking you to participate in opening your world for a glimpse into another culture that is different from yet similar to your own. You may participate in this survey anonymously, or you may state your name.

Please write a paragraph or two about what you would want the world to understand about you. Then ask five questions of the other group about the issues you would most like to understand about your counterpart.

If you are a Saudi woman, the other group is American women. I encourage you to ask anything. What would you like to know about an American woman? About her life and culture?

You have the opportunity to be curious and intimate. Remember, you may remain anonymous.

If you are American, please write a paragraph or two about yourself, your culture, or both. Ask five questions of a Saudi woman about her life and culture. You, too, have the opportunity to be curious and intimate.

Please send your statements and questions to the following address: lucaslanguage@gmail.com Thank you for your contribution.

As you will read below, the responses I received were quite varied. The answers here are raw and unedited. You will first hear from Ann Olson, a professor at Heritage University in Toppenish, Washington.

Participant Profile from American Ann Olson (American #1)

I grew up in a small, rural farming community on the open Sisseton-Wahpeton Sioux Indian Reservation in northeastern South Dakota. I had friends, both girls and boys, who were Native American, and I was aware at an early age of the differences in class status that those friends experienced. We all commonly heard disparaging remarks and witnessed acts of discrimination and misunderstanding and simple ignorance. I left that area when I was eighteen. I married, traveled with my husband, earned three college degrees. In 1989, we came to live in Ellensburg, Washington, and began full-time teaching at Heritage University in

1993. I believe it was my unusual reservation background experience that made me such a good fit for Heritage's multicultural mission and location on the Yakama Nation Reservation.

The first Middle Eastern student I came to know at Heritage was a young woman from Iran whose brother was Chair of Business at Heritage. She spent hours daily in the Academic Skills Center where I tutored English and where she worked hard to learn spoken and written English while furthering her education in computer sciences. We spent an academic year working together closely and getting to know each other.

Our friendship attraction was immediate and mutual. We seemed able to communicate surely and easily despite the language barriers because we had so much in common, even down to little life details. For example, we both drink milk before we go to bed because of the shared belief that it just feels good and seems to make us sleep better.

I've lost contact with her since her brother changed positions and moved to Seattle, but would be so pleased to learn how she is now. She never talked much about why she left Iran, except to make it clear that her husband was not good to her and that she needed to keep her whereabouts a secret from him.

I understood, perhaps only from inferences, that she had been abused. I did not ask direct questions but let her divulge what information she felt comfortable in sharing. I never associated her abusive marriage with Middle Eastern life because at Heritage, it was quite common to work with women, both young and old, who were using education in order to change a negative life situation.

Participant Profile from a Saudi Arabian (Saudi Arabian #1)

I have been married for thirteen years. I have two children, a boy and a girl. I am an Arab woman with my insecurities and strengths. I am both a mother and a child. I spend my life trying to figure out who I am and who I am supposed to be, both culturally and personally. I play multiple roles.

I guess in the end, I am a woman like many others worldwide, and we each have a story and a voice. I guess you are right in that what is missing is a dialogue, because we really share a lot deep down inside as human females.

Here are my questions to an American woman.

Questions from a Saudi Arabian (SA1)

Question SA1-1

One of the major questions or issues I struggle with is how does it feel to be truly you? I mean, you make many of your own choices and have many options; you go off to live on your own and discover yourself. I understand that all people are influenced by their surroundings, but I guess I always question what it might be like if it was just me for once and not me as part of a family.

Response to Question SA1-1 from an American (A2)

Well we do not "just go off on our own," especially if we have families to take care of. For example, if we are married or have children, we must take others into consideration. Most likely, we wouldn't go anywhere on our own without them or without their agreement.

However, within the family unit, we make

many everyday decisions on our own what to make for dinner, what to do with the children after school (which activities should we attend or participate in), what to do on the weekend; here we will consult with our husbands and children, etc.

So when Americans talk about going off on our own, it is during the time period when we are a single entity either before marriage or after it has ended for whatever reason. As young single women, we may decide to move out of our parental home into a house with friends, move to a different city to live and work, or we may decide to travel for an extended period of time. We make many of these same decisions later in life as newly single (or single-again) entities. Whatever the situation, as single women independent of family strictures, what we do with our lives and where and how we live them are our decisions to make, and we generally make them in our own best interest. We usually choose our hearts' desires, and that generally leads to our going out on our own. Again, this is during our single periods before marriage or after its end, when our children, if any, are grown.

You are right that the ability to be our own persons must be a heady experience it is. However, this experience is paid for by having to be very responsible for ourselves and by realizing that we are truly on our own in matters of finance, fulfilling employment duties, resolving problems, coping with illness, and all manner of daily situations that can make life very trying.

On the other hand, being on our own doesn't preclude having family or friends with whom we share our joys and sorrows. Family and friends are very important to those of us on our own, just as they are to those of us who are living within tighter family borders. Friends and family may be even more important when on our own because we will need helping hands from time to time.

We do want to share our lives with people we care about. Being on our own doesn't necessarily mean being alone. It simply means that sometimes decisions are made more easily because we ourselves are the only ones who need to be considered in order to choose the most favorable option.

Question SA1-2

Are there cultural roles or expectations? Can they easily be overcome?

A2 Response to Question SA1-2

The historic cultural expectation that women would or should stay at home and raise the children has been supplanted these days by the expectation that women will work and partner with their men in providing financial resources to cover the material needs of the family. This expectation to contribute financially is added to the underlying expectation that the woman will be the emotional mainstay of the family the heart that keeps the bond of family strong. Happily, that expectation also exists for men and has become even stronger as women have insisted that men actively participate in family life.

Therefore, to answer the question, even though it is commonplace necessary, even for women to work outside of the home, a new insidious expectation has arisen to dictate the parameters of women's lives inside the home and out. Women must be perfect in every way, every day. It's the Super Mom syndrome.

This syndrome demands that women be the perfect wife, the perfect mother, and the perfect homemaker, while also being the perfect career woman. At work, the woman must be better than the best man doctor, lawyer, or candlestick-maker. Otherwise, the attitude may be that she must not be worth her salt, and what is she doing in the workplace anyway?

At home, the woman must be the perfect wife, never forgetting that her primary role is companion to her husband. She must also be the perfect mother if she doesn't want to be besieged by guilt and blame because she works outside the home.

The worst fault would be that she has a great career and is good at what she does. If that career demands long hours and much effort, the necessity of being a perfect wife, mother, and homemaker becomes stronger. Conversely, the responsibilities of the career/job demand that she be perfect as well. The employer has no sympathy for the duties of the perfect wife, mother, and homemaker. The job comes first.

The tension between career and family is very strong, and competition for the woman's loyalties is fierce. Many women are crushed emotionally and physically, but they carry on daily, unable to give up either privilege or burden, as the case may be. Some opt out of either situation, but most continue, carrying the banner of "I can do it all," which has become the commonplace expectation, the norm, for our future generations of women.

Question SA1-3

Do you ever feel that Western women are oversexualized or objectified by society?

A2 Response to Question SA1-3

Yes! That is the simplest answer. It is impossibly difficult, or even just impossible, to reach and maintain the images of beauty and worth that are presented by the media and by the arbiters of standards for work, home, and life in general. Beautiful women are constantly presented to the public eye in advertising always smiling, always happy, always alluring, and (this is the "sexified" part) always desirable. "Buy this product from this woman, and you will be beautiful, too." Or "you will have fun" or "you will be appreciated," etc. The man who buys a particular product advertised or presented by a beautiful woman will gain all the social status imagined from having such an object "you can be the lucky man in this happy scenario."

The sexified phenomenon is not limited to advertising. Smart, engaging women in television programs, magazines, public office, or other situations in public view are most often beautiful and sexy, or derided because they are not physically appealing.

Questions from an American (A2)

Question A2-1

I think many Americans stereotype Arab or

Muslim women as being oppressed (seen as owned and controlled and not necessarily loved by men in their culture). How accurate is this stereotype in describing your experience?

Response to Question A2-1 from a Saudi Arabian (SA2)

I must make it clear that I cannot speak for all Arab women. I am but one Arab woman with my own experiences. I personally felt very loved by the men in my family. I guess the issue is in what you mean by controlled. As a daughter I had rules to follow, and as a wife I know my boundaries, so does that constitute control? I don't think so. I think it signifies love and respect. So this stereotype is wrong in my experience, but then again I come from what is considered an open-minded family that plays a major role.

Question A2-2

How accurate is this idea of being oppressed in describing the experience of your mother, sisters, or aunts?

SA2 Response to Question A2-2

In talking about other women in my life, my mother is a regular mom who, after thirty plus years of marriage, is constantly annoyed by my father.

My sisters are newly married and very happy.

They have never mentioned that they feel controlled or oppressed.

I only have one aunt who is divorced. I would guess that she was not controlled.

Question A2-3

What are your friends' experiences like?

SA1 Response to Question A2-3

My friends have different experiences. Some are happy and some are not, but I don't believe any of them ever felt oppressed. We all had hopes and dreams, and some even achieved them.

Question A2-4

How do you personally view your relationship with your husband or mate? How do you view your relationship with the other men in your family?

SA1 Response to Question A2-4

I am very happy with my husband, but like any other couple, we fight and argue but then make up. My relationships with the other men in my family are also good.

Question A2-5

How do you view your relationship with men as friends (if this is possible)?

SA1 Response to Question A2-5

I have some men as friends, but they are not Arab, just because that's how it worked out.

Participant Profile from an American (A3)

I am a fifty-seven-year-old American woman who has no children. I was married to a man twenty-two years older than myself who died twenty years ago. Then I met my current partner. We are not married, but we share a home and live as husband and wife. I have worked most of my life, primarily for the US government. I hope to stop work and live off my savings in a few years. My mom is ninety years old, and I help her quite a bit. My siblings, nieces, nephews, and a few good friends mean a lot to me.

I was raised by loving parents in a conservative religious environment (Roman Catholic). I matured in the 1970s. This era was very open sexually and politically. I enjoyed the cultural changes, but at the same time I felt a lot of guilt and uncertainty about how my choices would affect my future and whether they were moral.

Questions from an American (A3)

Question A3-1

In your Arab culture, if a woman reached menopause and did not have any children, how would she be viewed, with pity or acceptance?

Would it be assumed that she must have a medical problem affecting reproduction?

Response from a Saudi Arabian (SA2)

SA2 Response to Question A3-1

The question applies to married women who have reached menopause without children, as the vast majority of single Muslim women, particularly in conservative societies, do not engage in sexual activities if not married.

For those who are married without children, they are often pitied for (a) not experiencing motherhood, (b) living with the possibility of the husband taking a second wife who will bear him children, (c) not benefiting from her children's support in her older years, or (d) living deprived of motherhood because of her choice to live with a sterile husband. In my years, I have seen little evidence about acceptance of a couple that has no children. Social norms and family pressure for reproduction are very intense. This is not to say there aren't couples who continue their marriages despite not having children, but they often endure pity from people around them.

In the distant past and in the absence of medical tests, the wife was the *de facto* reason for not having children. In more recent years, families are a bit more open about the party to blame, although discussions about the issue are limited and happen in closed circles and opaque terms.

Nevertheless, childless women tend to stick with their husbands much more than the other way around.

Question A3-2

What happens to a woman in Saudi Arabia if her husband dies when she is thirty-six years old? Would she be likely to remarry? How would she meet men at this point?

SA2 Response to Question A3-2

In Gulf Cooperation Council (GCC) countries in general and in Saudi Arabia in particular, widows and divorcees tend to remarry. A second marriage for a woman here is much easier than a first marriage for a single woman who has passed the marriage years (i.e., her thirties).

I never understood this, but some attribute this to the fact that a second marriage for a woman is a second chance, and she is likely to work harder on her marriage (assuming she is a divorcee, of course). Others feel that men who marry widows or divorcees do so because they feel those women have real experiences in married life and are likely to succeed more together.

More often than not, these are marriages arranged by family members or friends. For women who are working, suitors may come from the work environment or contacts. Social forums have started to play a role in matching couples, but this is still very limited.

It is not unusual for some widows or divorcees to dedicate themselves to their children and refuse to remarry. There could be several reasons for this, but the well-being of children tops the list. Some are wary of bringing a husband who may not settle down well with the children; others are concerned about losing custody to the family of the dead or ex-husband when the children reach puberty. I do not have statistics on either scenario, but based on people around me, I would say the scale is balanced.

Question A3-3

Do women in Saudi Arabia look at Western styles

of women's fashions and wish that they could dress that way? Or do they feel sorry for Western women who seem to be compelled to get attention as sex objects every time they go out in public?

SA2 Response to Question A3-3

In terms of style, I believe our women are flush with choices, thanks to our malls, Internet, satellite TV, vacations abroad, and creative minds! Our women dress the way they like inside their homes, with family, and among female friends. The black *abaya* hides everything when in public or in mixed company. At parties or weddings, you are likely to see the same fashion trends as in other places, excluding extremes, of course. Most of our women do not feel the need or urge to dress to catch attention in public. There are exceptions, but most would be happy to enjoy their femininity and charm with just their husbands. Most women dress conservatively when in public but are more liberal in the privacy of their homes and with their husbands.

Moreover, there is certainly an aversion to women being on display or presenting themselves as sex objects. More sophisticated women may be more tolerant to such behaviors in other societies and may not express their objection in words; however, they do hold similar values.

Question A3-4

Do you feel that if a woman dresses in a certain way (low-cut blouse, short skirt) that a man cannot help but be strongly focused on a desire to touch or have sex with her rather than focus on her mind or personality? Do you think this is the fault of the man or based on biology?

SA2 Response to Question A3-4

There is a saying, "I am so focused on your actions that I can hear what you say." With freedom comes responsibility. We are brought up to believe that men would respond to visual and verbal stimuli. Hence, it should not be a surprise if men focus on their desires if they find themselves in situations where their manhood is being tested, deliberately or otherwise. If a woman wishes a man to focus on her mind or personality, she should dress up her mind and dress down her body.

Just like we keep our most valuable assets in safes or our jewels inside velvet wrapping, our bodies should also be cherished. This is not to be confused with the tradition of wearing an *abaya* in public. We tend to wear an *abaya* in Saudi or GCC countries largely for conformity and anonymity. When we do not wear them in public like when we are abroad we do dress much more conservatively compared to people in other parts of the world.

Question A3-5

Do you think rules of society and laws are a good reflection of how much power a woman has within that society? Or do women have subtle ways of influencing situations and getting their needs met that coexist with, and override at times, laws that place them in a lower position and limit their power? For example, the power to bind and influence husbands and children with love, and the power to influence husbands with sexual expression, as well.

SA2 Response to Question A3-5

Country laws and regulations—and even corporate policies—should focus on rights and obligations of a citizen irrespective of gender, thus they become a reflection of the power—and responsibilities—of one *human being* in that country.

Upon this foundation come additional laws to fulfill the vision of the country and its values related to the rights of women, children, parents, laborers, minorities, and so forth in specific scenarios.

I am not aware of specific laws against Saudi women's participation or engagement in society. However, the brevity in some laws or clauses has been interpreted or exploited to suit current social norms, mind-sets, and attitudes toward women.

Women have made up for current deficiencies through education, perseverance, family support, networking connections, and performance. For most women who have reached a high position in the public or private sector, family support from fathers, brothers, or husbands is the common thread.

The love and devotion from children is a given, as we all are indebted to our mothers. For Muslims, a mother's status is unique and her influence is tremendous. Mothers' blessings are lifelong goals for all men and women.

Much of the influence of our women is implicit and not confrontational. The skills of pampering, negotiation, persuasion, conflict management, enforcement, and many more are practiced in abundance. We are taught at a young age that we can get almost anything from our husbands if we know when and how to ask. This is far superior to reciting our rights under the law! In a Saudi household, we do not listen to the typical rhetoric; we focus on outcomes.

Life for women is much smoother than some Western media make of it, but it is yet to reach full, balanced empowerment.

Participant Profile from a Saudi Arabian (SA3)

I am a Saudi professional woman. I am married, with one son. I did my university degree in the United Kingdom in the early eighties and have worked for a single organization since 1985. When I joined, I was the only woman in the organization for a very long time, and I have worked my way up to reach executive management. My recipe is simple: succeed so others may follow. I worked with fellow countrymen just like the next man. I never thought of my gender and never brought it to work with me. I cherish our values and am proud to be Saudi.

Holding the stick from the middle (balancing praise with criticism) has helped me to advance at a pace that is rewarding to me and not too alarming to the conservative lot around me. At work, I am as competitive as any C-level executive in the United States.

At home, I live by the same values and habits of my mother and grandmother. I am the queen of the house, so I treat my husband as a king. I balance my time between my profession, my son, and my family, especially my parents. There is a lot that can be told about our society and our life, but unfortunately, much of what gets printed is sketchy, biased, or inaccurate.

Questions from a Saudi Woman (SA3)

Question SA3-1

Do you really feel unappreciated as a woman or a mother or a daughter because you're forced to become financially independent at a young age?

Response from Two American Women (A4 and A5)

A4 Response to Question SA3-1

I married for love at age eighteen, and my husband and I went off into our lives as best friends/lovers. He had to go into the military because he was the last one from our county to be drafted for the Vietnam Conflict, so the army supported us financially for our first three years together. After that we lived as students, very much like hippies, with few possessions and only part-time income as tutors and teaching assistants (TAs). We were young and childfree for the first ten years of our marriage. We traveled and studied and hiked mountains not settling down to children and full-time teaching positions until we were in our thirties.

I don't really even know any women (friends or family) of my generation who were forced to become financially independent. However, my daughter, who is thirty and has been married for four years, might answer this differently. I remember her saying that she and her friends felt pressured to graduate and get good jobs before marriage which she did.

A5 Response to Question SA3-1

"Unappreciated" is not the word I would use to describe financial independence at seventeen years old. "Difficult" is the more appropriate word.

There is a freedom to making your own decisions at any age. You suffer the consequences and reap the rewards. It is difficult to get ahead and secure your future without money. Women are more likely to depend on the wrong man because we are vulnerable at that age.

Question SA3-2

Do you feel it's more difficult to raise children because of the constant peer pressure in an open society? How do you handle that at home?

A4 Response to Question SA3-2

Good question! Because I grew up in the same "constant peer pressure" of our American society,

I'm not sure that it's any more pressure today on our children than we experienced back in the fifties, sixties, and seventies.

My daughter had a very rough time with "mean girls" just going into junior high, between fifth and sixth grade. These girls said they were her friends, but they worked behind the scenes to negatively affect her perceptions of herself—they were not good friends at all.

When she finally broke away from that group, it took courage, and she was alone and depressed for a while. We could see this at home and offered as much support as an eleven- or twelve-year-old will take from her parents. But she gradually found an excellent group of better friends, who continue to meet for friend and holiday get-togethers even now when they are all past thirty.

Question SA3-3

I think that American culture is highly exposed to the world through the media, but do you think there is any area in American culture that is terribly misrepresented to the world?

A4 Response to Question SA3-3

I think that American culture is stereotyped in the media. We are presented as a culture in which everyone drives new, fast cars while they play with the most advanced "techno toys;" women look like skinny fashion models with not enough clothes on and too much makeup; and everyone drinks coffee or fancy alcohol while talking about the stock exchange. If this is the media exposure that you mean, then it has very little to do with the life I live.

I feel that if someone from a Middle Eastern country were to meet me, he or she would be disappointed in how uncool and underexposed my real life is. My Honda is nine years old and usually unwashed. My cell phone is two years old, and I only know how to use about 15 percent of its functions. I am a middle-aged, average-weight woman with white or gray hair who is still wearing clothes that have been in the closet for more than twenty years. (If you wait long enough, everything comes back into fashion eventually!)

My life is based on the simple pleasures of getting together with my grown children, walking my dog in the evenings, and going to the pool for exercise. When we go out for dinner, my husband and I usually take a bottle of wine and picnic by the river that's our favorite restaurant!

Participant profile from American Carrie Aldrich (CA)

Carrie Aldrich has an MA in applied linguistics from the University of Alaska–Fairbanks, and bachelor's degrees in sociology and secondary English education from Indiana University. She is currently a first-year PhD student in the Language,

Literacy, and Culture Program at the University of Iowa. She taught a variety of literacy-based courses at the University of Alaska Fairbanks, including work with rural campuses.

Questions from Carrie Aldrich to a Saudi Arabian (SA4)

Question CA-1

Where do babies and children sleep in your house and why?

SA4 Response to Question CA-1

Up to the age of two years old, children usually sleep in our room. They are easier to take care of and safer there. After that, in a room near our room, so they can learn to be independent, and they should knock on the door if they need anything at night.

Question CA-2

How long do you breastfeed your babies?

SA4 Response to Question CA-2

I breastfed my babies for six months each, then I chose to go back to work.

Question CA-3

What are characteristics of a good husband?

SA4 Response to Question CA-3

A good husband should be caring, trustworthy.

Family should be his most important priority.

Question CA-4

Who does the laundry in the house?

SA4 Response to Question CA-4

Because I am working, I have a maid to do that,

with my guidance.

Question CA-5

Who folds the laundry and puts it away?

SA4 Response to Question CA-5

The maid.

Participant Profile from a Saudi Arabian (SA5)

I am a thirty-seven-year-old Saudi lady. I am married. I have two daughters: four and twelve years old. Since I was in the eighth grade, I dreamed about being a doctor. Then this dream grew bigger, and I decided to be an OB/GYN specialist to help women, because most of them are embarrassed to be examined. I define myself as a caring wife and mother and a helpful doctor to women in my society.

Participant Profile from American Muslim

Sahar Afi Abdur-Rahman (AR)

My name is Sahar Afi Abdur-Rahman. I am a thirty-three-year-old American Muslim woman. I was born and raised in Baltimore, Maryland, in an African American Muslim household. Although my name is completely Arabic and I studied Arabic as a foreign language since childhood, primarily for religious reasons, I have no other ethnic ties to the ethnicity. I am a sister, wife, mother, daughter, educator, and linguist. I love to read and to learn about other cultures.

Something that I believe is a bit unique about being an American Muslim, especially one from a nonimmigrant American perspective, is the way that we integrate into US society. My parents very much valued both education and Islam equally, and they sacrificed to ensure that their children were provided with tools to not only be successful as adults in mainstream society but also religiously. In order to achieve this, they and other Muslim educators and parents began schools or homeschooled their children. I am the only one of my siblings to have never attended a public school.

As a teenager, so that I could gain greater fluency in Arabic, I left home to study in Syria, where I stayed for two years. This was my introduction to being an adult and coming into my own identity. I mention this part of my life because, strangely enough, before going to Syria, I didn't truly have a realization of how very American I was and how much I love and cherish this identity.

Questions from Afi Abdur-Rahman (AR) to a Saudi Arabian (SA5)

Question AR-1

How do you define yourself as a woman and a member of society?

SA5 Response to Question AR-1

I define myself as a caring wife and mother and a helpful doctor to women in my society.

Question AR-2

What are the greatest challenges you face being a woman in Saudi Arabia?

SA5 Response to Question AR-2

The greatest challenge is how most people still look at my being a doctor as a humiliating job for a woman, because a woman would need to work with males in that specialty. People humiliate woman doctors because they believe women should only work with women and not males.

Another challenge is male domination in our society and the weakness women show in regard to this.

Question AR-3

I love to sit out in nature. How are you able to find a peaceful reprieve?

SA5 Response to Question AR-3

About the sitting outside, we have many gardens in each neighborhood, and also many Saudis have their family gatherings in a private place outside of Riyadh.

Questions from an American (A6) to a Saudi Arabian (SA6)

Question A6-1

Do you play sports?

SA6 Response to Question A6-1

Yes, I do. Swimming is my favorite.

Question A6-2

What is important for the world to understand about Arab women?

SA6 Response to Question A6-2

Arab woman are not a public case. We are human beings. Whatever we have in our lives, nobody has the right to decide and choose our destiny and change our religion and traditions.

Question A6-3

What do you want that you can't have?

SA6 Response to Question A6-3

I personally need nothing. Thank Allah, the women in my society also need nothing. Thank Allah, we have more than we need.

Question A6-4

Did you have a choice of whom you wanted to marry? Was it arranged for you?

SA6 Response to Question A6-4

Yes, I have the right to deny or accept the man who applies to marry me. Yes, it was arranged.

Question A6-5

What is your marriage life like?

SA6 Response to Question A6-5

Seriously, I have a good life with my husband and children. Like most Saudi women, I am the leader of my home; as are my sisters.

Question A6-6

How do you feel about covering your face and body?

SA6 Response to Question A6-6

Very comfortable. In our religion, we have the choice to uncover our faces, but it will be better to cover.

Questions from a Saudi Arabian (SA-7) to an American (A7)

Question SA7-1

Do Western women have the best life they can imagine?

A7 Response to Question SA7-1

No. I am very lucky about a lot of things. If I work, I can earn enough to have most things I need. I am traveling and seeing the world and meeting all kinds of people. I am able to follow my passions. In a lot of ways, I am very lucky. Western women have the ability to do whatever they want.

What stops this from being the best life is that

it isn't free. Our lifestyle comes at an enormous environmental and social cost. What I have, others don't, and the earth is being destroyed in the process. For example, I enjoy the luxury of driving, but every time I do, I pollute the environment. To me, this stops my life from being the best, but it is pretty good.

Question SA7-2

If you met Arab women, and especially Saudi women, what is the most interesting thing you would like to know about us?

A7 Response to question SA7-2

I would like to know how you feel about being told

what to do. I am completely my own boss. I am traveling through Europe alone right now. I've lived alone, and I've supported myself. I can't stand it when anyone tells me what to do. How do you feel about having to get permission from your father or husband or brother in order to do things? Would you like to have that system changed?

Question SA7-3

Do you accept a negative result of having your daughter have a boyfriend at a young age?

Response to Question SA7-3 from a

Forty-Eight-Year-Old American (A8)

As a mother, I have to weigh the advantages and

disadvantages of being open to all aspects of relationships for my daughter. I do not kid myself I do not control my daughter, and I have never controlled her. But sexual relationships open the heart/emotional self to possibilities of joy and pain, and I only want joy for my daughter. So it is sometimes difficult to allow freedom for my child. I feel her vulnerability.

I do not expect my daughter's relationships to be negative. I hope for all aspects of relationships for her to experience. The age of the girl having a boyfriend can only be controlled for so long in American society. I would like my daughter to wait until she is as emotionally mature as possible, but sexual hormones and natural rebellion play a part of her decision.

Educating a daughter and being open to all questions regarding relationships is a good policy. Personally, by the time I was thirteen years old, my friends were having sex. I felt pressure to lie to my friends about my sexual activity. I told them I had a secret boyfriend, when I did not.

Questions from a Saudi Arabian (SA8) to a Navajo American (NA)

Question SA8-1

Do Native Americans have a fair life in their motherland, which is now the United States?

Response to Question SA8-1

We have it better than those who now come to the United States as immigrants and minorities of this country.

There are over 550 different tribes, and each has sovereign rights from treaties signed with the federal government in exchange for taking our lands over two hundred years ago. This means we define for ourselves, as tribal nations, how to provide for our tribal members.

Many tribes have the ability to use casino or natural resource revenues to bring better health, housing, education, and jobs to our communities. But not all tribes have casinos or revenues from natural resources, and state governments fight tribes to block casinos or put up bureaucratic red tape as tribes negotiate for their revenues.

No other ethnic group in the United States can use this status, as we were the first inhabitants of this country, and the treaties that were negotiated with each tribe still hold true today.

As for Native American women, some tribes are matrilineal, and women have more power there than in those tribes which are patrilineal. For example, in my matrilineal tribe of the Navajo, women own the assets, livestock, and personal household property, along with rights to the children. If a couple splits, the husband typically walks away with just his personal possessions. Tribes that are patrilineal function like mainstream

US cultures, whereby couples work jointly or females defer to males for decisions.

Personally, I have an additional advantage because of clan systems established in our tribe. Some clans (totaling over sixty within the Navajo Tribe) are viewed as leadership clans. I was born into one of those first four clans that initially started the Navajo tribe. So whenever someone learns of my clan in introductions, there's recognition of my clan and I wield more status. I also have another advantage in that I am the great great granddaughter of Chief Manuelito, who was chief of our tribe when he signed the treaty with the US government in 1868. My last name of Manuelito is also recognized as that of my grandfather.

I hope this answer helps with some understanding about Native American people. It's hard to know in what context the Saudi woman is asking the question, and more explanations and history are necessary to fully answer questions. I hope that the world and its nation states can take the time to be educated about Native Americans.

Participant Profile from a Saudi Arabian (SA9)

I was born in a normal family who came from Mecca to Riyadh in the sixties. I got a free education. I got married when I was twenty years old, and then I finished my studies in 1997. I graduated from the Institute of Public

Administration in Riyadh while I was carrying my fourth child.

I had a dream to study engineering, but we didn't have this science for females at that time. I work as an administrative assistant in a famous medical college. Now, three of my eight children are studying in college. My hobby is art and drawing.

I like to know about other societies their history, language, tradition, religion, geography, and art. I can accept others' ideas if they're not against my religion. I like to deal and live with and have friendships with others, because our religion guides us to live in peace and deal in peace with non-Muslims and to follow the Islamic way.

I share with my husband every issue about my children and house. I have my own personality. I don't need his guidance unless I ask for his help. He must protect me, serve me in transportation, and finish the tasks that occur outside the home, these are rotten and boring but someone needs to do them.

In our society, there are many problems that can also be found in other countries, but the way we judge and punish is correct. What the bad people do never came from Islam. It happens because they are human beings. Jealousy, selfishness, cheating injustices are natural. That's why Islam came to control these things and stop bad behavior, just like Christianity and Jewish religions.

Saudis don't always fit the stereotypical views Westerns have of Saudi Arabia. Some Saudi Arabians have camels just for fun and some for trading. My family does not have oil, and we don't know where it goes, but we are doing fine. We are secure. My family and my country are safe, thank Allah.

I would like to add a very important point emotions are the biggest thing that controls our life, and our society is established on emotions. We have negative and positive issues.

I wish the policies that do not advance women would work faster and that the system would not control the specific people so it will be fairer.

In general, the universities in Saudi have an unfair system. They force you to study what you do not like and choose what you apply for without looking to your grades and desires.

Participant Profile from a Saudi Arabian (SA10)

Stating that I'm a Saudi woman often gets me a predictable reaction. I get sympathy and reserved curiosity. People stumble over their words as they try to form the questions they have in mind, while being careful not to offend. What they don't seem to understand is that being Saudi is a nationality, subject to a governmental system and laws.

It is part of any Saudi woman's identity, but it

is not the whole of her identity. It is the same as being American does not necessarily mean that a Mormon American woman in Provo, a Christian American woman in Dallas, and an Arab American woman born in Detroit would have even remotely the same life experience, despite being under the same government and laws. So when any Saudi woman writes about her experience as a Saudi woman, it is just that, her individual experience.

There are Saudi women whose liberal families shield them from the ultraconservative laws of the country, and there are women unfortunate enough to have been born to extremist families who take full advantage of the restrictions that the government allows them to impose on these women. And, of course, many fall into the spectrum between the two extremes.

Our issues in Saudi mostly have to do with changing the system. Women are not allowed to drive cars, they are subjected to a male guardianship system, and their employment opportunities are restricted.

Not being able to drive a car in a country lacking a public transportation system forces you to be at the mercy of male relatives or to pay a substantial amount of your income to import a foreigner to come and dedicate his life to chauffeuring you around. The male guardianship system ensures that many of your interactions with the government, such as obtaining a passport, going to court, and even having a major medical operation, hinges on how your guardian feels about the issue. Finally, employment restrictions make it difficult for you to follow your dreams and passions, and instead you have to fall on whatever you can get.

If American women are curious about the lives of Saudi women or even interested in helping Saudi women overcome their challenges, I suggest that they first educate themselves about the government and legal system of Saudi. They could even approach the issues as challenges that are similar to those that American women historically had to deal with. Having to deal with those issues in the past did not make the American women living before overcoming them homogeneous, exotic, or incomprehensible. Neither should the case be for Saudi women.

Questions from a Saudi Arabian (SA10) to an American (A9)

Question SA10-1

If you had to pick any Hollywood depiction (e.g. *Thelma and Louise*, *Desperate Housewives*, *The Good Wife*, etc.) to be the stereotype of an American woman, which one would you pick?

A9 Response to Question SA10-1

I can't stereotype the American woman even science has proven men are all the same, but women are different from one another. For instance, I have known Julie Lucas since 1991, and I have never met another woman like her ever in the United States or any other country. I have visited England, France, Germany, Italy, Spain, Switzerland, Denmark, Amsterdam, Morocco, Australia, Mexico, and Canada.

The only stereotype I have experienced with American women, compared to women in other countries I have visited, is that American women seem to be kinder to one another. When I worked in Germany and during my travels in Europe, I thought the women seemed to be frightened and distrustful of one another and the women were definitely openly rude to me.

I think American women have more
opportunities to explore what they want and who
they can be.

Question SA10-2

Are there any women's rights battles that still have
not been won in the United States?

A9 Response to Question SA10-2

Mothers will always have a disadvantage until
child support laws have teeth. (If a law has teeth, it
has the power to make people obey it). Over $100
billion in total is owed in unpaid child support.
This statistic comes from CNN.com. 2012 This
puts women and children at a huge disadvantage

and can leave a woman financially vulnerable for the rest of her life. I imagine child support laws and collection are just as equally weak or worse elsewhere in the world.

I think the issues women face all over the world could be changed if women supported and respected each other at home and in the workplace. Some of the worst things that have happened to women are not necessarily committed by men but by other women. Women are smart and strong and if we had each other's backs, we wouldn't be pondering this question.

Questions from a Saudi Arabian (SA11) to an American (A10)

Question SA11-1

As a mother, do you think it is OK for your daughter to have sex at a young age, and how do think you can protect her from this? If you think that having sex is freedom, don't you think that it is indecent?

A10 Response to Question SA11-1

I think that sex is a wonderful thing in a good relationship. When I was a child, we were taught that sex was really something to be ashamed of. Basically, the adults gave us the impression that sex was dirty and that women could not "enjoy" sex. That was really terrible, and I think it has led to many problems and even crimes.

But I do believe young people should wait to have sex until they are in a meaningful relationship and to also wait until they are older…later teen years.

Question SA11-2

Do you agree with the idea of separate schools for boys and girls? And why?

A10 Response to Question SA11-2

I think that separate schools can be OK, but I do believe that all boys and girls should attend school together at some point in their lives. I went to a primary school with boys and then high school with only girls and even one year of college with only girls.

My problem with high school was that the teachers did not insist that we girls learn math and science. They were trying to teach us to be educated mothers and not people who worked in the real world in interesting fields. We studied a lot of literature, history, and languages. As a result, I am afraid of math and science, even though I have tried to get over it.

Question SA11-3

Why do most American families kick their children out when they turn eighteen years old?

Why does their responsibility end there?

A10 Response to Question SA11-3

I do not think most families kick their kids out at age eighteen, though some do. Some Americans want their children to be independent. These days, because of the economy, many young-adult children are living with their parents because jobs are so hard to find for young people.

Some young people want to move out when they turn eighteen. I remember telling my parents, "I can't wait till I am eighteen and can move out of this house!" That comment hurt my parents very much.

Question SA11-4

If you see a Saudi Muslim woman covered in your

class or job, do you try to avoid being a friend with

her? Why or why not? Do you think that she has

an open mind or that she is behind the times?

A10 Response to Question SA11-4

No, I would not avoid the woman. I do find it

much easier to be around Muslim women who

only cover up their hair. The ones who cover their

whole face, except the eyes, are hard to relate to.

You can tell a great deal about people by the

expression on their face, so when you can't see the

face, you have to wonder what are they thinking. I

know that many women who are contemporary in

the Muslim world will cover hair and face. I have seen these women on TV and at demonstrations, as well as in the shops of stores when I visited Dubai.

Question SA11-5

How do you view Saudi women, since we have a very different culture and religion from you? Why do you think that most Saudi women are forced to do many things?

A10 Response to Question SA11-5

I am sure there are many different types of Saudi women. I am sure I could have a conversation with some and disagree and have a conversation with others and agree. I admire the Saudi women who are trying to get the right to drive a car. I don't know why Saudi women are forced to do things. They should not do things that they are opposed to. They should band together as sisters if they feel oppressed.

In America and Britain, women were denied the right to vote one hundred years ago. There were many demonstrations and acts of civil disobedience. The women banded together and pushed for their rights. Some men also joined the struggle.

Question SA11-6

Are you married and happy or not? Why do you change your name when you get married?

A10 Response to Question SA11-6

My husband died many years ago. I was happy, though we had some disagreements. I didn't change my name when I married. My husband encouraged me to do what I wanted. Later, I realized that he was sad that I did not take his name. That was sad for me, too, as I did not want to hurt his feelings.

Question SA11-7

Do you feel blessed because you're an American woman? And why?

A10 Response to Question SA11-7

Yes, in some ways, I feel lucky I was born in this

country, though we have many, *many* problems. This land is really beautiful "from sea to shining sea" beaches, mountains, swamps, deserts, farms, rolling hills, etc. We are lucky to have this land. It also helps us because the land naturally has water and minerals and the things people need in life.

We also have a pretty good Constitution, but sometimes I think we do not always follow the Constitution. But I am not prejudiced (I hope), as I think all women should be proud of the special things in their countries and with their cultures.

Participant Profile from a Saudi Arabian (SA12)

I am from Saudi Arabia and twenty-nine years old.

I am going to talk about my culture as a Saudi woman.

As Muslims, Islam defines our culture. All Saudi women can get an education what to do with the children after school, which activities should we attend or participate in. We will consult with our husbands and children about to do on the weekend.

In sex-segregated schools and universities. Saudi women mostly get married between the ages of twenty-five and thirty. The man proposes to her through her parents. All girls in Saudi culture live with their parents until they get married. Girls are not allowed to live alone.

Saudi women have to wear their hejab in public places such as shopping malls, restaurants, hospitals, and so on.

Although driving cars is forbidden for women, all Saudi families have a driver for the women. Freedom of women's movement is unlimited.

All kinds of jobs are open to women everywhere, except political jobs. So all women, after finishing their education, have the opportunity to work.

Saudi women are totally independent socially, financially, and educationally. Briefly, this is a simple view of Saudi female culture. Hopefully, I have given a clear vision of my culture.

Participant Profile from American Ayanna Estelle (AE)

I am twenty-one years old, a woman, and a recent college graduate living in Dallas, Texas. After graduating from college, I moved back home to live with my mom. I have noticed this is becoming the norm for Americans today. Many of the people that I graduated with are having difficulty finding jobs, and the jobs they do find do not pay enough to supplement a comfortable lifestyle.

I currently work full-time at an advertising agency in Dallas. I hope to continue working to gain experience, and hopefully in a year be promoted to a position that pays me enough so that I can live independently.

Participant Profile from a Saudi Arabian (SA13)

I'm nineteen, and I've just begun college. College life and post college life are very much the same here in Saudi. So hopefully I will be able to answer your questions.

Questions from Ayanna Estelle (AE) to a Saudi Arabian (SA13)

Question AE-1

What does a day-to-day life look like for a twenty-one-year-old Saudi woman?

SA13 Response to Question AE-1

The day-to-day life for a twenty-one-year-old woman here in Saudi, like I said, doesn't differ much from that of an eighteen-year-old or a twenty-three-year-old. If she has entered the workforce or is still completing her studies, her days would most probably follow one pattern: work/school, home, work/school, home.

There are not many activities outside of work that women can indulge in if any, they would only be once-a-month things.

Question AE-2

What is the average level of education obtained by an Arab woman?

SA13 Response to Question AE-2

I'm not quite sure about the average level, but I know one thing for certain. Education in Saudi is tough in terms of medicine, business, and engineering. I believe women focus on these majors in particular because they're the only majors a woman can be proud of and can be considered equal to her fellow male coworker.

Question AE-3

Is it normal for an adult woman to live at home with her parents?

SA13 Response to Question AE-3

Yes, extremely so. The only three conditions for a

Saudi woman to not live with her family are that she's studying abroad; she is married and living with her husband; or she is divorced and doesn't wish to move back in with her parents.

Question AE-4

Would you feel safe living alone?

SA13 Response to Question AE-4

Frankly, I don't know because it isn't the norm for a Saudi woman to live alone for no particular reason unless she is taking residence in a college campus or housing provided by a company she works for.

Question AE-5

What is a societal change that you have noticed recently?

SA13 Response to Question AE-5

In terms of women rights, there have been recent breakthroughs. Women lawyers are claiming their positions. Unfortunately, people associate the lack of women rights to Islamic law, which is far from the truth.

Questions from an American (A11) to a Saudi Arabian (SA14)

Question A11-1

Do you feel that if a woman dresses in a certain

way (low-cut blouse, short skirt) that the man cannot help but be strongly focused on a desire to touch or have sex with her, rather than on her mind or personality? Do you think this is the fault of man?

SA14 Response to Question A11-1

In this question, my answer will be different because we have different religion and rules. I will give you the answer from the point of view of religion first. The answer from the Quran, our holy book, says in Sutra 24:30–32, "The believing women are to reduce [some] of their vision and guard their private parts and not expose their adornment except that which [necessarily] appears thereof and to wrap [a portion of] their head covers

over their chests and not expose their adornment

except to their husbands, their fathers, their

husbands' fathers, their sons, their husbands' sons,

their brothers, their brothers' sons, their sisters'

sons, their women, that which their right hands

possess, or those male attendants having no

physical desire, or children who are not yet aware

of the private aspects of women. And let them not

stamp their feet to make known what they conceal

of their adornment. And turn to Allah in

repentance, all of you, O believers that you might

succeed."

Now, from my point of view, I don't think

that it is the fault of men. There are men

everywhere in the world, not only here in Saudi, whose innate sexual desires and instincts push them to focus on sexual relations. This proves that there is sexual harassment in all countries of the world.

Question A11-2

Should women drive in Riyadh? Why or why not?

SA14 Response to Question A11-2

I lived in the United States for four and a half years, and I didn't drive there, even though my husband gave me the choice. In my opinion, driving for women in Saudi is really not a good idea. Most Saudis have big families, so in each house usually there are at least five cars for the father and his sons, so the streets always have traffic. If women were to drive, the cars will be doubled on the road, and the traffic will be trouble. Second, Saudis would need a lot of preparation if they decided to let women drive. For example, they would need to establish driving schools for women, and all the staff should be women because of our culture.

We feel more comfortable by having drivers to drive us anywhere or riding with our fathers, brothers, or husbands. Also, if a woman drives, she will have more responsibilities than what she has now, such as taking kids to school and picking them up.

Question A11-3

How many children do you have? Are you happy?

SA14 Response to Question A11-3

I have three children, and I am happy in my life, thank God.

Question A11-4

Did you have a choice of whom you wanted to marry? Was it arranged for you? How did it go?

SA14 Response to Question A11-4

Yes. I had the choice of whom I wanted to marry. It was an arranged marriage but when a man asks my family to marry a woman, she can ask about him and meet with him with one of her family members present. Then she can choose whether she wants to marry him or not. This is what our religion taught us, and we are happy with it.

My marriage has gone really well. I have been married for ten years, and I am still happy.

Question A11-5

How do you feel about covering your face and body?

SA14 Response to Question A11-5

I have the choice to cover or not, and I choose to cover. I feel comfortable and happy because I am like a protected diamond—not anybody can touch or see it.

Participant Profile from a Saudi Arabian woman

I want the world to know that I am a proud Muslim woman. I am a normal, typical woman with feelings, emotions, dreams, desires, and the willpower to choose and own my own life. I have the freedom to live my life the way I like and do whatever I wish.

I also want the world to know that Saudi women have all rights but are not forced to take any responsibilities. I have a lovely family who encouraged me to be educated and to have a successful life. I have a bachelor's degree; I also have a master's degree from the United States. I am a full-time working woman and a mother at the same time.

Here in Saudi, we always have a strong relationship with our families. Even if the kids graduated from college, their parents are still responsible about them, and they take care of them. For example, now I have been married for ten years, and I still go to my family house almost every day. When our parents get older, we are responsible to look after them and take care of them. The parents usually go to live with one of their kids.

Question from an American (A12) to a Saudi Arabian (SA15)

Question A12-1

How do you define yourself?

SA15 Response to Question A12-1

I am a mother of two children whom I take care of all the time. I work in the morning at my home, working in my business until my kids and my husband come back from work and school. I am a queen in my world, my home. Outside my home, I have many things to do. Family gatherings and meeting friends are important.

Question from an American (A13) to a Saudi Arabian (SA16)

Question A13-1

How do you feel about Americans? Do you think that Americans are all alike?

SA16 Response to Question A13-1

People are not the same, and Americans are not an exception.

Question A13-2

Do you watch American or British TV shows? Which do you like better, American or British? Why?

SA16 Response to Question A13-2

I used to watch Oprah, Tyra Banks, and other TV Americans. But lately I stay away from TV shows in general, even the local ones. From time to time, I watch the *Ellen Show* on YouTube to cheer up.

Question A13-3

Do you think most people are interested in doing work to make a more peaceful world? Or do you think most people are too busy with their own problems to do much about peace?

SA16 Response to Question A13-3

Well, I think the economic issue the whole world

is facing, in particular the Middle East because of the Arab Spring, makes people more conscious about their future life in terms of living.

Question A13-4

Are you able to participate in political decisions in your country? Can you vote or be on a board or commission? Can you run for office? Over the last ten or fifteen years, have opportunities for women to participate in the political affairs of your country increased or not?

SA16 Response to Question A13-4

Participation in politics is very limited for us as Saudi women, but King Abdullah started the change for women to be more active in making

valuable decisions in the Council. My participation

involves social volunteer work only.

Question A13-5

Do you read fiction? Who are your favorite authors

or authors that you think are very good writers?

From what countries?

SA16 Response to Question A13-5

I read fiction, mainly classic. Jane Austen and

Paulo Coelho from Brazil.

Complex issues and fascinating thoughts and ideas

have been expressed here. We have opened

Pandora's box, indeed. We cannot assume, just because Muslim women dress a certain way, that they can't speak for themselves. Nor should we assume that because American women dress a different way, they could also be put in a box of stereotypical views. There are huge issues yet to be addressed. Issues like domestic violence, sex trafficking, and rape. Until we really talk to each other and learn who we are, not as American or Muslim people but as people, we will have no common ground on which to work.

I want to focus in the future on the cause of these problems so we can respond with real solutions. This book is only the beginning. Let's keep in mind the importance of a two-way conversation. I want to thank all the women who have asked and answered questions to promote communication. If we don't keep each other aware of what we see and learn in the world, how can we grow and understand our world?

I would love to hear from more people. Let's continue the conversation at www.lucaslanguage.com.

We all have a need to understand the world around us. Or we have the choice of letting go of the need to categorize as a way of understanding other people and places. First, I need to know myself. Understanding when judgments enter my mind and why they do helps me keep an open mind.

Some generalizations I feel safe holding on to. Joy is essential to life. Laughter is a necessary part of life. Strong positive, relationships full of love keep us sane.

Open Doors Fact Sheet:
Saudi Arabia Institute of International
Education Educational Exchange Data from
Open Doors 2012

Year	Number of Students From Saudi Arabia	Percentage of change from the previous year	Number of US Study Abroad Students Going to Saudi Arabia
2011/12	34,139	50.40%	0
2010/11	22,704	43.60%	18 (up 28.6%)
2009/10	15,810	24.90%	14 (down 46.2%)
2008/09	12,661	28.20%	26
2007/08	9,873	25.20%	2
2006/07	7,886	128.70%	1
2005/06	3,448	13.60%	3
2004/05	3,035	-13.80%	1
2003/04	3,521	-15.70%	2
2002/03	4,175	-25.20%	2
2001/02	5,579	5.80%	1
2000/01	5,273	2.30%	1
1999/00	5,156	4.60%	2
1998/99	4,931	7.90%	1
1997/98	4,571	-	1

In the 2011/12 academic years, 34,139 students

from Saudi Arabia were studying in the United

States (up 50.4 percent from the previous year). Saudi Arabia jumped two places to become the fourth leading place of origin for students coming to the United States, and is by a wide margin the first among Middle Eastern countries in terms of sending students to the United States.

Academic Level: The majority of Saudi Arabian students study at the undergraduate level. In 2011/12, their breakdown was as follows: 42 percent undergraduate; 18 percent graduate students; 38.7 percent other; 1.3 percent OPT (Optional Practical Training).

Historical Trends: In the late 1970s, the number

of Saudi students in the United States increased rapidly, peaking in 1980/81 with 10,440 students. After that, there was a period of fluctuation, until 1993/94, followed by increases until 2001/02. In the 2002/03 academic years, enrollments dropped 25 percent and continued to decline until 2005/06, when participants in the Saudi Scholarship Program began enrolling on US campuses. In 2005/06, the number of Saudi students in the United States rose 14 percent from the previous year, to a total of 3,448. With the scholarship program in place, the number of students showed a dramatic rise of 129 percent in 2006/07, when it appeared in the list of top twenty-five places of origin at number twelve, and continued to experience double-digit growth in the following four years. With scholarship students in the pipeline for several years, the increase reached 44 percent in 2010/11. Saudi Arabia has moved up to the fourth leading place of origin, from number six the previous year and number nine in 2008/09.

Note: Study abroad figures from Open Doors reflect credit given by US campuses during the survey year to their students who studied abroad in the academic year just completed, including the summer term.
Source: Open Doors: Annual Report on International Educational Exchange, published annually by IIE with support from the US Department of State's Bureau of Educational and Cultural Affairs.

Selected Resources

Abudi, Dalya. *Mothers and Daughters in Arab Women's Literature (Women and Gender: the Middle East and the Islamic World)*. BRILL, 2010.

Abu-Lughad, Lila. *Do Muslim Women Need Saving?* Cambridge, MA. Harvard University Press, 2013. Kindle Edition.

Ahmed, Leila. *Women and Gender in Islam: Historical Roots of a Modern Debate.* Yale University, 1992.

Alsanea, Rajaa. *Girls of Riyadh.* New York, New York. Penguin. 2005

Al-Shaykh, Hanan. *Women of Sand and Myrrh.* Trans. Catherine Cobham. New York. Anchor. 2013. Kindle Edition.

Ashour, Radwa, Ferial J. Ghazoul, and Hasna Reda-Mekdashi. *Arab Women Writers: A Critical Reference Guide*. 1873–1999. Trans. Mandy McClure. Cairo: The American University in Cairo Press, 2007. Print.

El Saadawi, Nawel. *The Hidden Face of Eve: Women in the Arab World.* London: ZED Books, 1980.

Fatany, Samar. *Saudi Women Towards A New Era.* KSA. Ghainaa Publications, 2007.

Hartman, Michelle. *Gender-Genre and the Missing Gazelle.* Feminist Studies Vol. 38.1, 2012

Mikhail, Mona. *Seen and Heard: A Century of Arab Women.* Northampton, MA. Interlink Publishing Group, 2003.

Moussa, Sabri. *Seeds of Corruption.* Trans. Mona Mikail. Interlink Pub. Group, 2002.

Naber, Nadine. *Arab America: Gender, Cultural Politics, and Activism Nation of Newcomers: Immigrant History as American History.* New York. NYU Press, 2012.

Rabab, Abdulhadi, Evelyn Alsultany, and Nadine Naber. *Arab and Arab American Feminisms: Gender Violence and Belonging.* Syracuse, New York. Syracuse UP. 2010. Print.

Sabry, Tarik. *Arab Cultural Studies. Mapping the Field.* IBTauris, 2012. Kindle Edition.

Said, Edward W. *"Embargoed Literature." Between Languages and Cultures: Translation and Cross-Cultural Texts.* Ed. Anurdha Dingwaney and Carol Maier. Pittsburgh: U of Pittsburgh P, 1995 (pages 97–102).

Zogby, James. *Arab Voices: What They Are Saying About Us and Why It Matters.* Palgrave. Macmillan, 2010.

Author's photograph: Ingrid Pape-Sheldon

Cover art by: Meshail Alkulib

www.ingramcontent.com/pod-product-compliance
Lightning Source LLC
Chambersburg PA
CBHW060355290526
45791CB00002B/519